I0880895

Welcome.

Welcome to your *We Learn from the Sun* teacher lesson plan. In this lesson plan, you will find classroom lesson plans, student activities, colouring pages and other amazing activities. Please feel free to adapt any or all activities to your students' age group.

All of these lessons have the approval of author David Bouchard.

Tables of Contents:

Lesson A - Getting to know *We Learn from the Sun* :

1) Read the book.

2) Facilitate Conversation :

- **Think, pair, share** : What do you know about the Sun? Have you ever seen a sun rise? Have you ever seen a sunset? What does it look like?

- **Think, pair, share** : What do think about the poetry in the book? Do you like it?

- **Class Brainstorm** : What is your favourite teaching from the sun that we learned from the book?

- **Group Work** : In small groups answer the following question, which animal did you like the most from the story?

- Read the book again having the students think about the following questions. How many animals were talked about or shown in the book? How many directions are there?

- **Class Brainstorm** : How many animals were talked or shown about in the book?
  (Answers : Wolf, Raven, Buffalo, Bear, Beaver, Turtle and Eagle)

  How many directions did you hear?
  (Answers : East, South, West, North, Sky, Earth and Heart)

- **Class Brainstorm** Color Activity : Have students fill in the next page with the appropriate colour associated with each direction.

Teacher Note: Use the last page in *We Learn from the Sun* for quick reference of the directions and their respective colours/animals.

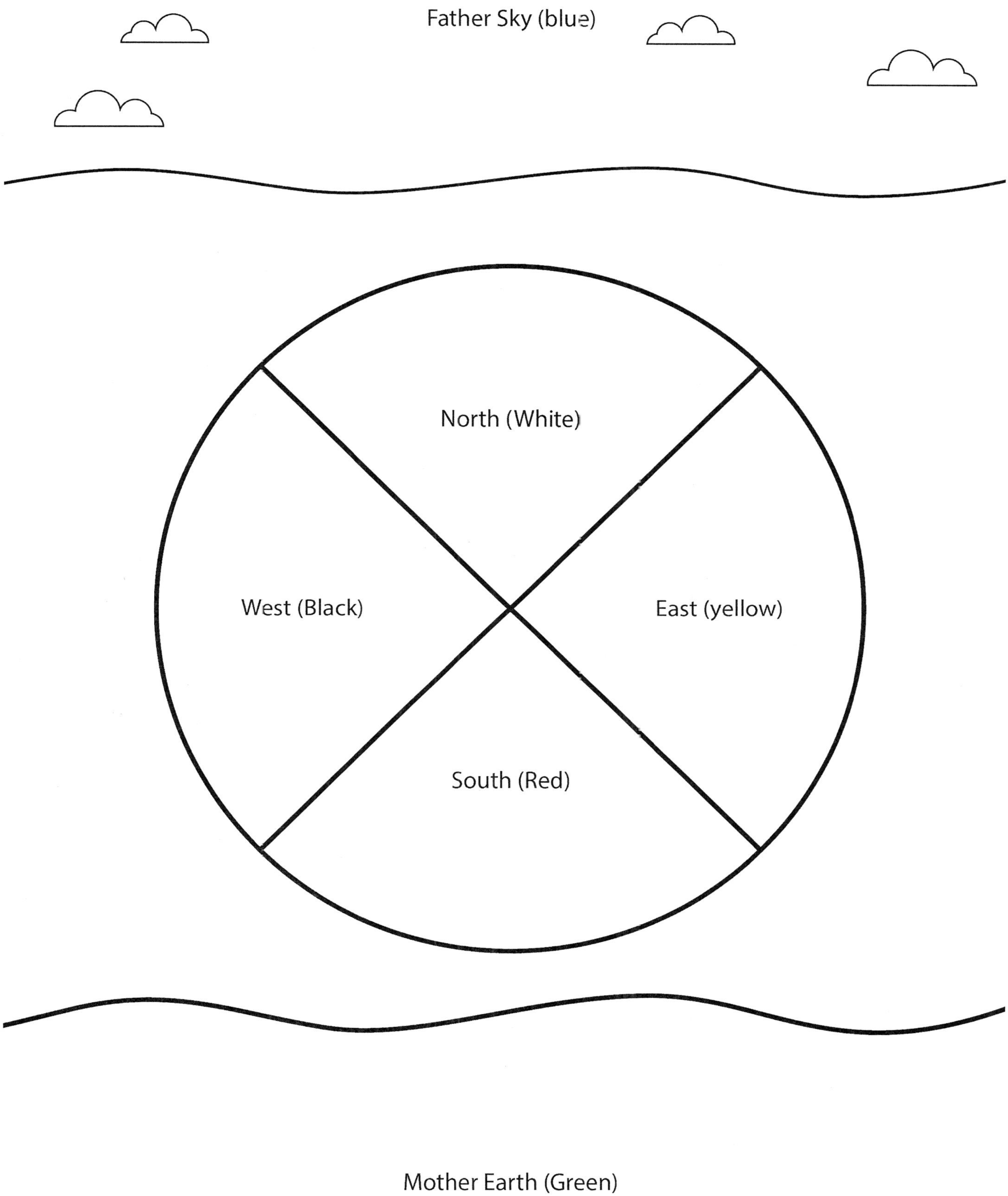
Father Sky (blue)
North (White)
West (Black)
East (yellow)
South (Red)
Mother Earth (Green)

Name: _____________

Place the words activity :

Place the words into the text. Reference words are provided in **Bold**.

First Sacred Teaching :
Words: **Wrong, East, Not**

The sun rises each day,
In the __________ as we pray.
It is huge, it is strong,
We are _______ big, that is ________.

Second Sacred Teaching :

Words: **Unique, South, Sun, Gifts**

When the Sun's ________ we see,
We have ________, you and me.
We're _________, everyone one,
We learn that from the ________.

Third Sacred Teaching :
Words: **Sun, Rest, West, Nest**

When we look to the ________,
Where the ______ goes to _________
We are taught to respect,
From the Old to the _________.

Fourth Sacred Teaching :
Words: **Bear, Courage, White, North**

Then we turn to the _________
And our ___________ comes forth.
________ and landscape are ________
We find strength to do right.

Fifth Sacred Teaching:
Words: **Wise, Father, Beaver**

Next, we turn our heads high
To our __________ the sky.
And hear __________ advise,
that we need to "be ________."

Sixth Sacred Teaching:
Words : **Down, Earth, Tree, Go**

We are told to look _________,
Mother _________ is the Ground
She's the _______ - she is snow
Where we're from - where we'll _____.

Seventh Sacred Teaching:
Words: **Love, Hearts, Deep**

When we look _________ inside,
In our _________ Eagle flies
She is up there above,
Teaching us how to _________.

Lesson B - Writing your own Poetry

Purpose : Have students engage with experimenting with poetry.

Please note: Typically it would not be acceptable for students to change an Indigenous person's writing. In this situation David Bouchard has given his approval for changing or experimenting with his words for educational purposes.

1) Read the book.

2) **Think, pair, share:** What do you like about poetry? Do you prefer a story in rhyme or not? Give one example of two words that rhyme.

3) **Class Brainstorm:** Write down the words that rhyme on the board using the book as reference point. When writing the words use blank lines before the rhyming word to show where the rest of words can go.

eg.
____________________ live
____________________ give

As a classroom have offer students to the words and offer this as a classroom example. Repeat the process 2-3 times with different examples.

4) Activity - Using the template on the following page have students write words to come up with their own poetry. If your students do not require the template please use their own paper.

Name: ________________

We Learn from the Sun Poetry Writing :

Feel in the sentence leading up to the rhyming word.
Please use your own page if you require more space.

1. ____ live

____ give.

2. ____ fun

____ sun.

3. ____ see

____ me.

4. ____ down

____ ground.

5. Come up with your own :

____

____.

Name:____________________

We Learn from the Sun

Fill in the lines with words from the poem.

Created using the Crossword Maker on TheTeachersCorner.net

cross

1. Colour associated with Father Sky.
2. Animal from the South that teaches Honesty. Hint: Black bird.
5. Last sacred teaching and associated with the Eagle.
6. Colour associated with the heart and the Eagle.
8. Animal associated with the East. hint- They travel in packs.
11. Animal associated with the Bear and North.
12. Where does the sun rise?
15. Colour associated with the Wolf and Mother Earth.
17. Colour associated with Mother Earth and the Turtle.
18. Colour associated with Raven and Honesty.

Down

1. Animal associated with Courage from the North.
3. She flies above all things teaching us how to love.
4. Represents Mother Earth. Hint: Has a shell.
7. Colour associated with the Buffalo and West.
9. Animal that builds dams. Represents Father Sky and Wisdom
10. Animal that represents West and Respect.
13. We learn from the __________.
14. How many teachings and directions are there?
16. Colour associated with Bear and the North.

Name: ____________________

Word Search:

We Learn from the Sun

```
                    Y M G
               S K L O E R V V P
           Q C M P D U Y T R H W X F
        Z Z J V N S M E S B H L O X Z D C
      U U J M R I E L S U Z Q P F N C E L I
    E T H M K W K L V U L N E F A R E R T O O
    A F Q I R D O V T A R B O T I E Q S X I Z
  U S S Q E X W L H R M R Z R G C S L P T L H V
  F T B L R E P J I L M Z V M O Z P I T X Y E W
O D H E N E R H O L A F F U B G P E U K R H A P T
Q O U P K Z F N Y N G V H T K E X C O T I U R C E
K H T R A E E T F B O J G O S V X T S H O M T A V
R N W G P X L D R R N B W P F B S H N Q E R C Y P D H
T P U W M V J L U S Q L G N Y Q U O U R T L A T R D R
S H C K O C L T T G C A N F N P D N U P V B B D E J S
P I E E Q G P H K V C H T R O N A G T Y M I M B N
Q U R R E C W E R O K I M F I E T A K H G I C U Z
P Z Z E E L G X A C Z S X L P S E E G A R U O C H
  H O N U V P Z B G W D G O E M Z W Y J E D X U
  G L I V H A R K E L D X W I E W C E Y E L P Q
    A J G R D E U L A E Y K N N E V Y C N O V
    W E S J U H B P N R U C U Q O U E Z B T E
      B K E S T P B B X C S W L X D L R Z B
        Y R G O C J C Z J Q Y Y K K K B T
           W M Q U O I Y Q S H P Z I
               Y E K P N S B L P
                    B O U
```

SUN
WOLF
HUMBLE
YELLOW
EAST
RAVEN
HONESTY
RED
SOUTH
BUFFALO
BLACK
RESPECT
WEST
BEAR
WHITE
COURAGE
NORTH
BEAVER
WISDOM
BLUE
SKY
MOTHER
EARTH
TURTLE
GREEN
TRUTH
EAGLE
LOVE
PURPLE
HEART

Name:__________________

Circle and Match :

Circle the direction, then draw lines between the direction with its corresponding the animal and colour. See example.

West (Respect)	Raven	White
East (Humility)	Eagle	Purple
Our Heart (Love)	Bear	Green
South (Honesty)	Buffalo	Blue
Father Sky (Wisdom)	Turtle	Yellow
North (Courage)	Beaver	Red
Mother Earth (Truth)	Wolf	Black

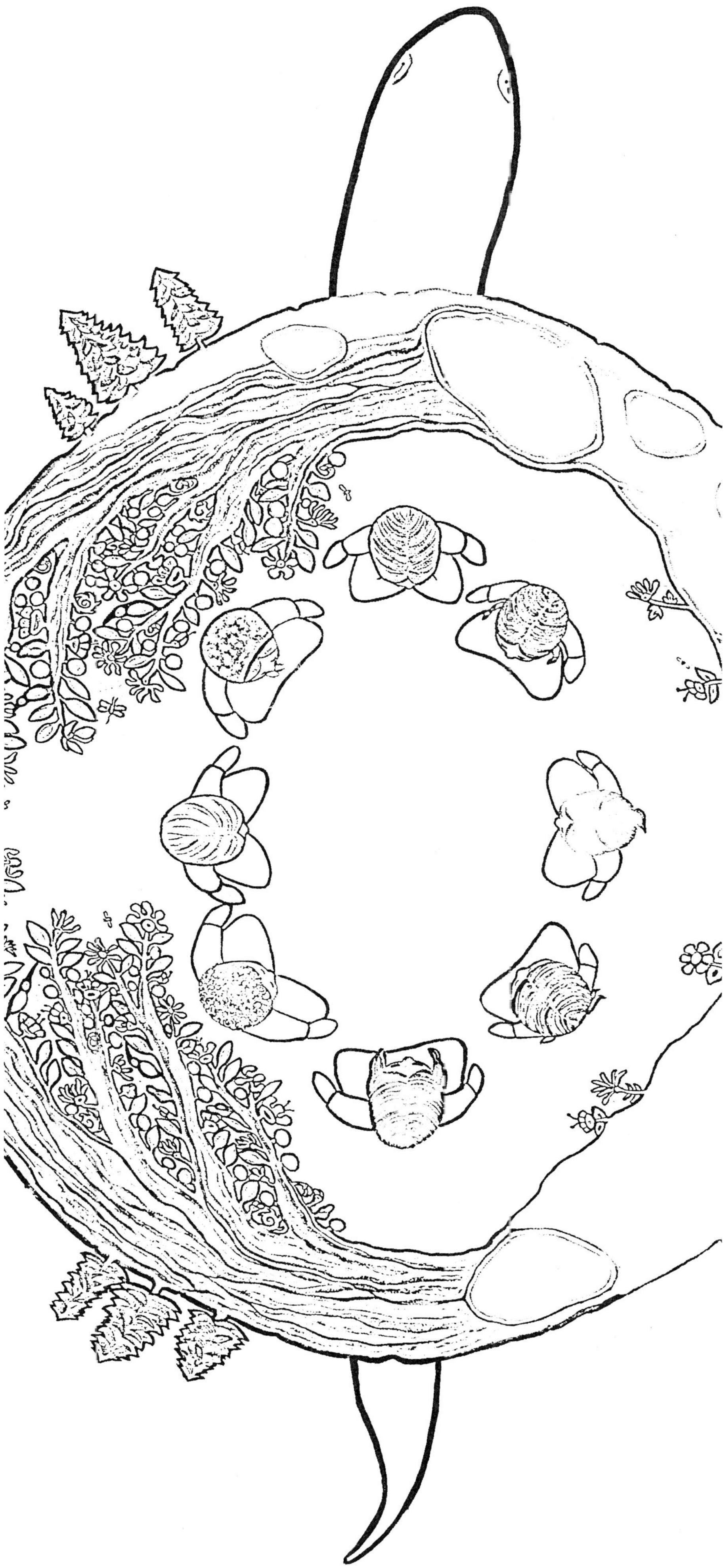